HISTORY IN ART

TUDOR ENGLAND

Raintree

NICOLA BARBER

www.raintreepublishers.co.uk
Visit our website to find out more information about **Raintree** books.

To order:
☎ Phone 44 (0) 1865 888112
▤ Send a fax to 44 (0) 1865 314091
▢ Visit the Raintree Bookshop at **www.raintreepublishers.co.uk** to browse our catalogue and order online.

Produced for Raintree by
White-Thomson Publishing Ltd
Bridgewater Business Centre, 210 High Street,
Lewes, East Sussex, BN7 2NH.

First published in Great Britain by Raintree,
Halley Court, Jordan Hill, Oxford OX2 8EJ,
part of Harcourt Education.
Raintree is a registered trademark of Harcourt Education Ltd.

Editorial: Kelly Davis and Diyan Leake
Consultant: Alexandra Gajda, New College, Oxford
Design: Michelle Lisseter and Richard Parker
Page make-up: Mind's Eye Design Ltd, Lewes
Picture Research: Elaine Fuoco-Lang
Map artwork: Encompass Graphics
Production: Kevin Blackman
Originated by Dot Gradations
Printed and bound in Hong Kong, China
by South China Printing Company

ISBN 1 844 43372 2
09 08 07 06 05
10 9 8 7 6 5 4 3 2 1

British Library Cataloguing in Publication Data
Barber, Nicola
History in Art: Tudor England
709.4'2'09031
A full catalogue record for this book is available from the
British Library.

Acknowledgements
The publishers would like to thank the following for permission
to reproduce photographs (t = top, b = bottom):
Alamy p. **33** (l) (Howard Taylor); Art Archive pp. **7** (Musée du
Château de Versailles/Dagli Orti), **10** (Palazzo Barberini,
Rome/Dagli Orti), **11** (Musée du Château de Versailles/Dagli Orti),
13 (Travelsite/Jarrold Publishing), **14** (Museo del Prado,
Madrid/Dagli Orti), **29** (b) (Victoria & Albert Museum,
London/Eileen Tweedy), **32**, **35**, **36** (t) (Travelsite/Jarrold
Publishing), **39**, **40**, **41** (Travelsite/Jarrold Publishing), **44** (b);
Bridgeman Art Library pp. **3**, **4**, **12** (John Bethell), **16**, **17** (b)
(Society of Apothecaries), **17** (t) (Whitworth Art Gallery, The
University of Manchester), **18**, **20** (t) (Lauros/Giraudon), **21**, **22** (t)
(Hermitage, St Petersburg), **22** (b), **25** (Lauros/Giraudon), **26**, **27**,
28, **30**, **34**, **36** (b), **37** (The Stapleton Collection), **38**, **42**, **43**, **45**;
Corbis pp. **8** (Angelo Hornak), **19** (t) (Kit Houghton); Fotomas p.
15 (The Fotomas Index); Mary Evans Picture Library pp. **5** (t), **5**
(b), **19** (b), **24** (b), **29** (t); National Maritime Museum p. **23**; By
Courtesy of the National Portrait Gallery, London p. **9**; TopFoto
pp. **6** (TopFoto.co.uk), **20** (b) (TopFoto.co.uk/English Heritage), **31**
(TopFoto.co.uk), **33** (r) (Topham/Fotomas); Victoria & Albert
Picture Library p. **24** (t).

Cover photograph of a portrait of an unknown man by Isaac
Oliver (c.1565–1617) reproduced with permission of Bridgeman.

Every effort has been made to contact copyright holders of any
material reproduced in this book. Any omissions will be rectified
in subsequent printings if notice is given to the publishers.

Disclaimer
All the Internet addresses (URLs) given in this book were valid at
the time of going to press. However, due to the dynamic nature of
the Internet, some addresses may have changed, or sites may have
changed or ceased to exist since publication. While the author, the
packager and publishers regret any inconvenience this may cause
readers, no responsibility for any such changes can be accepted by
either the author, the packager or the publishers.

The paper used to print this book comes from sustainable resources.

Contents

Chapter 1   History and art   4
Art as evidence   6

Chapter 2   The Tudor period   8
Henry VIII   10
Architecture   12
Edward VI and Mary I   14
Elizabeth I   16

Chapter 3   The Tudor world   18
Going to war   20
Seafaring and exploration   22
New trade   24
Portrait painting   26

Chapter 4   Everyday life   28
Costume and fashion   30
Education   32
Popular entertainments   34
Gardens   36
Literature and music   38

Chapter 5   Religion   40
Protestant reforms   42

Timeline   44
Glossary   46
Further resources   47
Index   48

Words included in the glossary are in **bold** the first time they appear in each chapter.

History and art

The Tudor period was born of conflict, when Henry Tudor defeated Richard III at the Battle of Bosworth in 1485. King Henry VII, the first Tudor, was succeeded by his son, Henry VIII, who became one of the most famous English monarchs. After Henry's death, three of his children – Edward, Mary and Elizabeth – came to the throne in turn. The Tudor **dynasty** ended with the death of Elizabeth I in 1603.

▼ Henry VIII brought a sculptor called Pietro Torrigiano from Florence in Italy to build a magnificent tomb for his father. This was the first example of Renaissance art in England.

The Renaissance

During the Tudor period, literature, music, architecture, portrait painting and theatre all flourished in England, particularly during the long reign of Elizabeth I. This artistic activity was part of the **Renaissance** – a revival in learning and culture that took place across Europe. The Renaissance started in Italy in the 14th century as people began to study the art and writings of ancient Greece and Rome. The achievements of the ancient Greeks and Romans had been virtually unknown since the decline of the Roman Empire in the 5th century. The new ideas that arose from these studies inspired artists in Italy such as Michelangelo and Leonardo da Vinci, and writers such as Dante Alighieri. The ideas of the Renaissance spread northwards during the 15th and 16th centuries.

Humanism

The Renaissance influenced artists, writers and scholars. It led to **humanism**, a new way of looking at the world that celebrated the intelligence and achievements of humans.

The screen surrounding the tomb is English, made by Thomas Ducheman

The delicacy and skill of the modelling, and the lifelike features, are typical features of Renaissance art

The base of the tomb is made from black and white marble

The figures of Henry VII and his wife Elizabeth of York are made from bronze covered with a fine layer of gold

Humanists such as Desiderius Erasmus, the most famous scholar of the 16th century, also developed new ideas about the nature of Christianity which challenged the **Roman Catholic Church**. In the Middle Ages, the Catholic Church was extremely powerful across Europe. Some humanists questioned the authority of the **pope**, the head of the Catholic Church, and some important Catholic teachings such as how the human soul reached heaven after death.

◄ Desiderius Erasmus (right) was a humanist scholar. Opposite him sits the French humanist Gilbertus Cognatus.

The Renaissance prince

Henry VIII was known throughout Europe as a prince of the Renaissance. He was well educated, a fine musician and poet, and a gifted athlete. He was surrounded by a glittering court, and he employed artists and craftspeople from all over Europe to work in his palaces. One of them, Nonsuch Palace in Surrey, no longer stands but pictures show an impressive building lavishly decorated in the Renaissance style.

Printing

One development that helped the spread of Renaissance ideas was printing. Johannes Gutenberg set up the first printing press in Europe in the middle of the 15th century. An English wool merchant called William Caxton learned the techniques of printing while he was working in Bruges in Flanders, now part of Belgium. When he returned to England in 1476, Caxton set up the first English printing press. This invention brought a gradual increase in the number of books available.

▼ Nonsuch was built as a huge and splendid hunting lodge for Henry VIII to celebrate the 30th anniversary of his accession. Work was started on the palace in 1538, and it was still unfinished on Henry's death in 1547. The palace was sold to the Earl of Arundel by Mary I, who disliked hunting. However, Elizabeth I often visited the palace on her summer journeys, and towards the end of her reign it became a royal palace once more.

The walls and towers were decorated with representations of scenes from Greek myths. The scenes were carved in a type of white plaster called stucco, and the timbers enclosing the stucco panels were gilded to create a dazzling effect

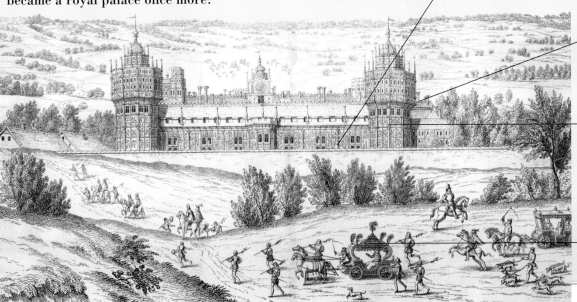

This view shows the south side of the palace

The huge corner towers were octagonal in shape

This engraving, by Hoefnagel, shows Elizabeth I on her way to Nonsuch in 1582

5

Art as evidence

Many art treasures survive from the Tudor period. They range from tiny items of jewellery to full-length paintings, from pieces of elaborate embroidery to complete buildings. All these objects tell us something about the Tudors and how they lived. However, it is useful to ask some questions about this evidence.

Who created these objects, and who were they made for? We know the names of many of the artists and craftspeople who worked at the courts of Tudor monarchs. Influenced by the revival of learning and culture in Europe, the Tudors employed many artists and craftspeople from outside England. Some of them, such as the painter Hans Holbein the Younger, were well known throughout Europe. The Tudor monarchs were important **patrons** of the arts, commissioning paintings, buildings and other works of art. Wealthy, powerful people, such as Cardinal Wolsey, Henry VIII's most influential minister, also spent vast amounts on buildings and furnishings.

Paintings

A number of Tudor paintings depict scenes that give us information about different aspects of Tudor life. For instance, according to popular belief, monarchs could cure their subjects of various diseases, including scrofula – a disease of the skin – and **tuberculosis**, by touching. People believed that this gift was only possessed by monarchs and was a sign of their right to govern the country.

▼ The ability to heal sufferers from scrofula and tubercular diseases by touch was known as 'touching for the King's (or Queen's) Evil'. People believed that this power was held by all the English monarchs.

Mary I is shown touching a sufferer

In many Tudor paintings, particularly portraits, every part of the picture has a special significance which Tudor onlookers would have understood. For example, by portraying Elizabeth I with a rainbow, the artist is linking the Queen with the sun – the Latin words on the left confirm this. In addition, the flowers on her dress, the serpent on her arm, and the jewel on her ruff are all **emblems**, with symbolic meanings. Once these elements are understood, the picture can be seen as a statement about Elizabeth as Queen – she is the bringer of peace, love and wisdom. Many Tudor paintings carry symbolic 'messages' such as these.

The art of the woodcut

Many books of the Tudor period were illustrated with **woodcuts** (see example on page 24). These were made by cutting away areas of a block of wood to leave a raised design. The artist coated the uncut parts of the wood with ink. When a sheet of paper was pressed on to the block, the cut areas came out white, while the uncut areas printed the design on to the paper. The block could be re-inked and used over and over again to repeat the image. Woodcut illustrations give us important information about the lives of ordinary people in Tudor times.

▼ The 'Rainbow portrait' of Elizabeth I was painted at the end of the Queen's reign, in about 1600, probably by the Flemish painter Marcus Gheeraerts.

The jewel on Elizabeth's ruff is an emblem, showing the Queen's role as the heroine of all her courtly knights

The Latin words 'Non sine Sole Iris' mean 'No Rainbow without the Sun'. Elizabeth is the sun who brings the rainbow after a storm – and by implication the bringer of peace

The bodice of Elizabeth's dress is embroidered with spring flowers, showing that Elizabeth brings the warmth and renewal of springtime after the dark and cold of winter

The ears and eyes on Elizabeth's cloak symbolize the need for a wise queen to know what is happening in her kingdom, through intelligence gathered by her loyal officials

The jewelled serpent on Elizabeth's sleeve stands for wisdom; the heart hanging from the serpent's mouth stands for love

The Tudor period

In August 1485 Richard III was killed, and Henry Tudor became Henry VII, King of England. Richard's death brought to an end 30 years of unrest caused by the rival claims of the houses of Lancaster and York to the English throne. The coronation of Henry VII marked the final victory of the House of Lancaster and the beginning of the Tudor **dynasty**, which was to last until the death of Elizabeth I, more than a hundred years later.

▼ Work began on Henry VII's chapel in Westminster Abbey in 1502–3. The architect was probably Robert Vertue, one of the King's master masons.

Henry Tudor

Henry VII was descended from an old Welsh family, the Tudors, on his father's side, and from John of Gaunt, Duke of Lancaster, on his mother's side. He was brought up in Wales, but in 1471 he fled to France, where he lived in exile until 1485. During this time the House of York ruled England, with Edward IV, Edward V and Richard III as Yorkish kings. As head of the House of Lancaster, Henry Tudor was the last hope for Lancastrian supporters. However, Henry's attempt to seize power would have been hopeless if he had not had the support of the French king when he sailed from France to Wales in August 1485. With 4000 French soldiers and his own followers, Henry overwhelmed Richard's forces at the Battle of Bosworth.

Above the stalls is a series of carvings of saints

*The banners show the **emblems** of famous knights*

Some of the stalls (covered seats) around the edge of the chapel date from when the chapel was built. Others were added in 1725

Henry never forgot his Welsh background and upbringing. He called his elder son Arthur after the legendary **Celtic** king. He flew the Welsh red dragon on his **standard** during the Battle of Bosworth. And the Welsh dragon appears in the **heraldic** sculpture and stained-glass windows inside the chapel at King's College, Cambridge.

The first Tudor king

The new king married the daughter of Edward IV, Elizabeth of York. This marriage brought together the houses of Lancaster and York, and made future rivalry less likely. Portraits of Henry VII show a shrewd-looking man. He encouraged trade, avoided going to war, and left the country in a prosperous state at his death. He also greatly increased his own income by reorganizing royal financial affairs. But he gained a reputation for being mean with money, and few mourned his death in 1509.

▼ Map of Tudor England and Wales showing places mentioned in the text.

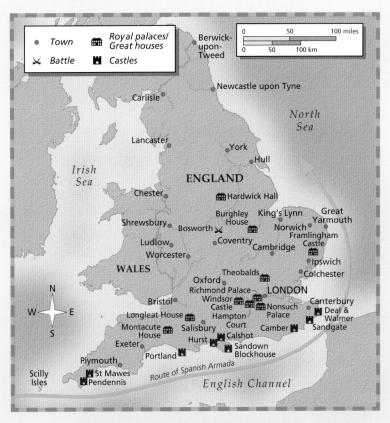

● Town	🏛 Royal palaces/ Great houses	
✗ Battle	🏰 Castles	

0   50   100 miles
0   50   100 km

Berwick-upon-Tweed

Carlisle
Newcastle upon Tyne

North Sea

Lancaster
York
Hull

Irish Sea
ENGLAND

Chester
Hardwick Hall

Shrewsbury
Burghley House
King's Lynn
Great Yarmouth
Bosworth ✗
Norwich
Framlingham Castle
Ludlow
Coventry
Cambridge
Worcester
Ipswich

WALES
Theobalds
Colchester

Oxford
Richmond Palace
LONDON
Bristol
Windsor Castle
Nonsuch Palace
Canterbury
Longleat House
Hampton Court
Deal & Walmer
Sandgate
Montacute House
Salisbury
Camber
Exeter
Hurst
Calshot
Sandown Blockhouse
Plymouth
Portland
Route of Spanish Armada
Scilly Isles
St Mawes
Pendennis
English Channel

N
W ✦ E
S

▼ This portrait of Henry VII is probably by a Flemish artist, William Sittow. After the death of Elizabeth of York, in 1503, Henry looked for a second wife. The portrait was painted as part of the unsuccessful negotiations for a match with Margaret of Austria, daughter of the Holy Roman Emperor, Maxmilian I.

A contemporary account of Henry VII described his eyes as 'small and blue', his teeth as 'few, poor and blackish', his hair as 'thin and white' and his complexion as 'sallow'

In his right hand, Henry holds a red Lancastrian rose

White and red roses

The various battles fought between the Yorkists and the Lancastrians from the 1450s to 1485 later became known as the Wars of the Roses. This name came from the symbols adopted by the two sides – the white rose of York and the red rose of Lancaster. The white rose was used as an emblem by the Yorkists during the reigns of Edward IV and Richard III. However, the red rose became associated with the Lancastrians only after Henry Tudor became king. When Henry VII married Elizabeth of York, the union of the two rival houses was represented in paintings showing the white and red roses side-by-side.

The inscription records that the portrait was painted on 29 October 1505 by order of Herman Rinck, a representative of the Holy Roman Emperor, Maximilian I

Henry VIII

Henry VII's elder son, Arthur, died in 1502 at the age of 15, so when Henry VII died it was his younger son, Henry, who succeeded him. The sickly young Arthur had been married to a Spanish princess, Catherine of Aragon. In order to continue this important alliance between England and Spain, Henry VIII married his brother's widow. Henry looked forward to the birth of a male heir but although he and Catherine had several children, none survived beyond infancy except for one – a girl named Mary.

In 1526 Henry fell in love with one of Catherine's ladies-in-waiting, Anne Boleyn. Henry became determined to marry Anne, but to do this he needed the head of the Roman Catholic Church, the **Pope**, to declare his marriage to Catherine invalid. When the Pope refused to do this, Henry declared that the Church in England was independent of Rome, and made himself 'Protector and supreme head of the Church and clergy in England'. This break from Rome was part of the **Reformation** (see page 40). In 1533, he and Anne were married and in the same year Anne had a daughter named Elizabeth.

Henry soon tired of Anne, and she was executed in 1536. He went on to marry four more wives, only one of whom produced a male heir. Jane Seymour had a healthy boy in 1537, named Edward, but Jane herself died as a result of the childbirth.

◄ This portrait of Henry VIII is a copy from a famous mural painted by Henry's court painter, Hans Holbein, in 1537. The mural was painted on the wall of Whitehall Palace. Sadly the palace was destroyed by fire in 1698.

Henry's broad body was made to look even more massive and powerful by the exaggerated shoulders of his clothing

The King wears a heavy shoulder chain encrusted with jewels

Henry's doublet is slashed to allow the lining beneath to show through, as was the fashion of the time

Leopards and panthers

The story of Henry's six wives can be traced in the decorations on Tudor royal buildings. When Henry married Anne Boleyn, the pomegranate (a type of fruit), representing Catherine of Aragon, was quickly replaced with Anne's emblems, including the falcon and the leopard. The fall of Anne meant that the leopards were changed into panthers – emblem of Jane Seymour. However, with so many rapid and costly changes, it is not surprising that some emblemswere overlooked or simply left alone. For example, the beautiful carved wooden screen in King's College Chapel in Cambridge still bears the initials 'H' and 'A', for 'Henry' and 'Anne', as well as Anne's falcon.

The Field of the Cloth of Gold

In 1520, Henry VIII met the French king, Francis I, near Ardres in northern France. The sumptuous meeting became known as the Field of the Cloth of Gold. Its purpose was to celebrate the recent alliance between France and England, made in 1518. The entire English court sailed to France for this occasion – five thousand courtiers dressed in their finest clothes. Another two thousand to three thousand people erected their lavish tents. Food, cutlery, crockery and other provisions also crossed the Channel. However, the alliance was short-lived. The following year, Henry signed a treaty with the Spanish emperor, Charles V, and by 1522 France and England were once more at war.

▶ Henry VIII arriving at the Field of the Cloth of Gold. The artist who painted this rather fanciful interpretation of the events of June 1520 is unknown.

The latest gunpowder technology was used to make a firework dragon which flew across the sky at the end of the festivities

Henry VIII and the French king, Francis I, took part in a wrestling match. Henry VIII lost

Elaborate tents and pavilions housed some of the events

A royal salute was fired by the cannon in this castle as Henry VIII rode past

Henry VIII rides on a white horse, surrounded by his courtiers. His chief minister, Cardinal Wolsey, rides next to him

Architecture

Although the first Tudor monarch, Henry VII, had a reputation for meanness, he was nevertheless a great patron of architecture. He built royal palaces in Richmond (west of London) and Greenwich (east of London), but he is remembered for his religious buildings. He ordered the completion of the chapel at King's College, Cambridge, which had been started in the 1440s during the reign of Henry VI. He also completed St George's Chapel at Windsor Castle. In 1503, work started to add a lavishly decorated new chapel at Westminster Abbey in London. This chapel was originally built to house the tomb of Henry VI. Instead, it was to become the burial place of Henry VII himself.

Henry VIII's palaces

Henry VIII is remembered for the huge number of palaces he built and maintained all over England. At the time of his death he owned over fifty grand houses and palaces. One of the finest was Hampton Court Palace (in west London). This was built for Henry's minister, Cardinal Wolsey, who fell from favour when he failed to achieve a separation for Henry from Catherine of Aragon. Wolsey died in 1529, and Henry took over his splendid house, extending it and making it even more impressive.

▼ Hardwick Hall in Derbyshire was built for Elizabeth, Countess of Shrewsbury, known as Bess of Hardwick. Construction of the hall began in 1591.

The huge windows stretch almost from floor to ceiling on every floor. Glass was expensive, so large windows were an indication of status

The initials 'ES' stand on the parapets of the hall, flaunting Bess of Hardwick's power and wealth for all to see

Between 1536 and 1540, Henry closed down the Catholic monasteries in England (see page 41), and used some of the money from them for his grandest project, Nonsuch Palace. Unfortunately, nothing survives of the palace today, but paintings and descriptions give us an idea of the scale of this building. Henry wanted Nonsuch to rival a chateau (French castle) called Chambord built by the French king, Francis I. Work began on Nonsuch in 1538, and many craftspeople came from Europe to work on its decoration and furnishings. The palace was demolished in about 1682.

Elizabethan houses

Although Elizabeth herself built very little during her reign, many of the leading figures of her court put up large houses. Some of the best known, including Longleat House, Montacute and Burghley House, still stand today. Many of these houses were built not only as homes for their owners, but also as places fit to receive the royal court. Every year, Elizabeth I went on a royal **progress** through the countryside. On these progresses, she and her court stayed at the houses of local nobles. No expense was spared, and many older houses were specially extended or improved in preparation for a royal visit.

The outside is decorated with simple lozenge shapes on the first floor, and more intricate lozenge patterns on the second floor

A balcony runs along the length of the first floor

Timber frames

Many manorhouses, farmhouses and townhouses that survive from the Tudor period are timber-framed. In places where wood was plentiful, timber was the cheapest material for building. These areas included south-eastern England, the west Midlands and Cheshire. The Feather's Hotel in Ludlow is a good example of this type of building.

▼ The Feather's Hotel in Ludlow, Shropshire, was built in 1603.

The timber frame is painted black, while the brick and plasterwork infill is white

Edward VI and Mary I

Edward VI was only nine when his father, Henry VIII, died in 1547. For the first two years of his short reign, Edward was in the hands of his uncle and guardian, the Duke of Somerset, known as the 'Lord **Protector**'. Edward had been brought up in the Protestant faith and Somerset was also a staunch Protestant. Between them, they set about turning England into a truly Protestant country.

In 1549 Somerset was overthrown by the Protestant Duke of Northumberland. When Northumberland saw that the young king was becoming increasingly ill, possibly with **tuberculosis**, he began to scheme to keep Edward's half-sister Mary from the throne. The daughter of Henry VIII and Catherine of Aragon, Mary was a devout Catholic. Edward VI died in 1553 and Northumberland put his own Protestant daughter-in-law, Lady Jane Grey, on the throne.

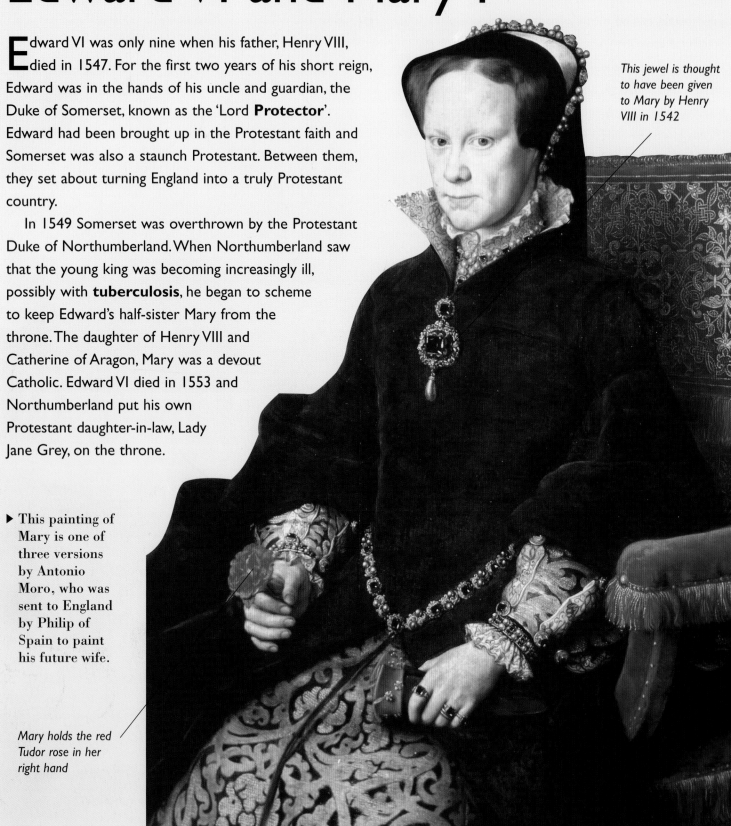

This jewel is thought to have been given to Mary by Henry VIII in 1542

▶ This painting of Mary is one of three versions by Antonio Moro, who was sent to England by Philip of Spain to paint his future wife.

Mary holds the red Tudor rose in her right hand

Lady Jane was the grand-daughter of Henry VIII's sister Margaret. Edward had been persuaded by the Duke of Northumberland to name Jane as his successor, but Jane's reign lasted only nine days. Mary gathered forces around her at Framlingham Castle, in East Anglia, and marched to London, where she was declared Queen.

Mary I

Mary did her best to undo the Protestant reforms of Henry VIII and Edward VI. England became a Catholic country once more, and many Protestants were persecuted. Some were burned at the stake for their faith, including Thomas Cranmer, who had been made Archbishop of Canterbury.

Mary married Philip II of Spain in 1554, and hoped to produce heirs to continue the Catholic line, but she remained childless. She was devoted to Philip. However, Philip only married her because he saw their union as a useful political alliance. He remained in England for just a year after their marriage before returning to Spain. Mary died in 1558 after a short reign, and was succeeded by her half-sister Elizabeth.

Somerset House

When the Duke of Somerset became Lord Protector, he immediately began to build a palace suitable for his new, high rank. The Duke owned land in London between the River Thames and the Strand. It was here that he began building his great mansion, Somerset House, in 1547. However, clearing the site required the demolition of a number of churches and chapels. This was an extremely unpopular move which led to his imprisonment in the Tower of London in 1549, although he soon obtained his release. The palace was completed in 1551, but the Duke had little time to enjoy it before he was imprisoned and executed for treason the following year. His high-handed style of politics, his methods of dealing with various uprisings during Edward's reign, and the ambitions of the Duke of Northumberland all contributed to his downfall.

▼ To many contemporaries, the construction of Somerset House symbolized the greed of 'Protector' Somerset.

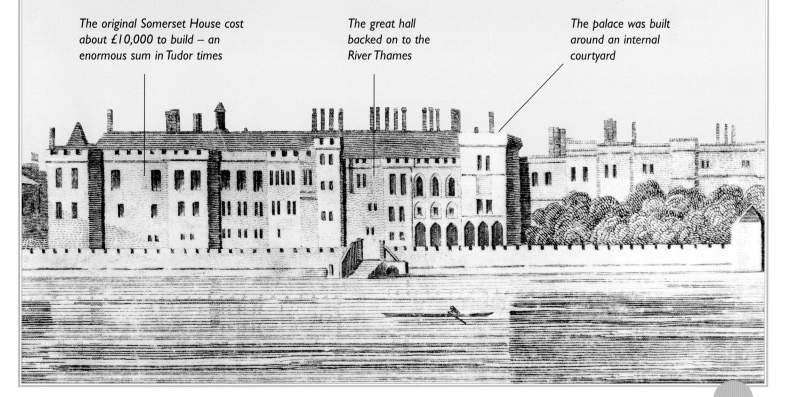

The original Somerset House cost about £10,000 to build – an enormous sum in Tudor times

The great hall backed on to the River Thames

The palace was built around an internal courtyard

Elizabeth I

During the reign of Elizabeth I, England became a peaceful, stable Protestant country once again, with Elizabeth positioned safely at the head of the English Church.

From the day she came to the throne, the new queen understood the importance of winning her subjects' loyalty. Elizabeth decided not to marry, even though remaining childless would cause problems with the succession after her death. Instead she reigned as the 'Virgin Queen', dedicated to her country. Each year she travelled around England on a royal progress, visiting different country houses, towns and villages. At every stage, she was entertained and welcomed with lavish ceremonies. These journeys allowed ordinary people to see their queen.

Portraits of the Queen

Hundreds of portraits of Elizabeth were painted during her reign, most of them displaying her as a powerful monarch, wearing sumptuous clothes and brilliant jewels. Many of the objects in these pictures have symbolic meanings. For example, in one portrait Elizabeth wears a jewel in the shape of a pelican. The pelican was believed to peck its own breast to draw blood to feed its young. This symbol showed that Elizabeth would sacrifice herself for her country. Only a few of these pictures were painted from life – most artists copied images of the Queen. As Elizabeth grew older and her beauty faded, she took care to ensure that portraits continued to show her as a youthful – and still powerful – woman.

Elizabeth sits in a raised chair, protected by a canopy carried by several of her courtiers

Elizabeth wears a magnificent, jewelled white dress

▶ *Queen Elizabeth going in Procession to Blackfriars in 1600. This painting is probably by the artist Robert Peake. It shows Elizabeth surrounded by her courtiers, possibly on her way to a wedding, although exactly what is happening in this picture remains a mystery.*

This is the sword of state in a red scabbard (sword cover)

The ladies of Elizabeth's court follow behind

16

The Catholic threat

During Elizabeth's reign, the main threats came from the Catholic countries of France and Spain, as well as Catholics in England itself who wanted to replace Protestant Elizabeth with a Catholic monarch. In 1569 there was a Catholic uprising in the north of England, and two years later a plot was discovered to put Mary Queen of Scots on the English throne. Plots to replace Elizabeth with Mary and restore Catholicism continued until the death of the Scottish queen. In 1588, Philip II of Spain sent a large fleet, the Spanish Armada, to attack England (see page 21).

Mary Queen of Scots

Mary Queen of Scots was the daughter of James V of Scotland and the French princess Mary of Guise. Her grandmother was Margaret, sister of Henry VIII, and it was this that gave her a right to claim the English throne. Mary spent her childhood at the French court and at 15 was married to the French *dauphin* (heir). When he died she returned to Scotland. After a disastrous second marriage, she fled to England in 1568. Although Elizabeth imprisoned her, Mary became the focus of Catholic plots against the Queen. After 19 years, Elizabeth had Mary executed, in 1587.

◀ This 19th-century painting shows a romanticized view of the scene just before the execution of Mary Queen of Scots, in 1587.

Elizabeth and her troops are shown watching from the English shore

▲ This depiction of the Spanish Armada was painted by an unknown artist. The picture shows the Battle of Gravelines, which took place on 29 July 1588 and was the decisive moment when the Armada was finally put to flight.

This ship is the first Ark Royal of the British naval fleet, commanded by Lord Howard of Effingham

The Tudor world

Tudor art and architecture tell us a great deal about the Tudor world. Portraits of monarchs and their courtiers provide a unique pictorial record of the period. Buildings such as castles remind us that Tudor England had to be defended from its Catholic enemies. Objects brought back from foreign lands by seafarers give us an insight into the world beyond English shores.

The Tudor court

Life at the Tudor court revolved around the monarch. The courtiers closest to the king or queen looked after his or her everyday needs as well as providing entertainment. Some of these courtiers were also members of the government who advised the king or queen on matters of policy. Hans Holbein the Younger painted portraits of some of the most influential figures at the court of Henry VIII, such as Sir Thomas More and Thomas Cromwell. He also drew many lesser figures, including Sir Thomas Boleyn, father of Anne, and Thomas Wyatt, a poet who was Henry's rival for Anne's affections.

▼ Elizabeth I at a Maundy Thursday ceremony, painted by Levina Teerlinc.

Elizabeth washed the feet of poor women, in imitation of Jesus Christ at the Last Supper, when he washed the feet of his disciples. The number of women who had their feet washed corresponded each year to Elizabeth's age

This painting shows a youthful Elizabeth in the early years of her reign, around 1560

In the early part of his reign, Henry VIII had little time for matters of state, preferring instead to spend his time hunting, **jousting**, playing tennis, dancing and feasting. He left the running of the country to his trusted Lord Chancellor, Cardinal Wolsey. When Henry and Catherine of Aragon had a baby son in 1511, a grand tournament and pageant was organized to celebrate the birth of the heir. Henry himself rode in the jousts, in a coat embroidered in gold thread. Sadly, the baby boy died shortly after.

Henry spent large amounts of money on lavish court entertainments. Elizabeth also loved hunting, music and dancing, but she was more careful about her spending when she became monarch. She was an accomplished musician – a miniature painting by Nicholas Hilliard shows her playing a stringed instrument called a **lute** (see page 27). She was also an energetic dancer. Despite the disapproval of the **Puritans**, Elizabeth encouraged theatre productions, and in 1583 ordered the formation of her own dramatic company, the Queen's Men.

◀ A knight mounted on his armoured horse was an impressive sight.

Catherine of Aragon watches the joust with her ladies-in-waiting

As Henry VIII delivers a blow to his opponent, his lance shatters

▶ A tournament included jousting competitions, such as the one shown here. Two riders galloped towards each other holding long poles, called lances. The aim was to unseat an opponent with a blow of the lance.

Henry's coat and the covering on his horse are embroidered with the initials 'H' and 'K' for Henry and Catherine (Katharine)

The riders are separated by a wooden barrier to keep the horses apart

Going to war

Tudor monarchs had to protect themselves from rebellion at home, and from attack from overseas. Both Henry VII and Elizabeth I avoided going to war, believing that military conflict was a waste of money. In the early years of his reign, and later on, Henry VIII rode into battle against the French, despite the meeting at the Field of the Cloth of Gold in 1520 (see page 11), which briefly brought peace between the two countries.

◄ Henry VIII's flagship, the *Henry Grace à Dieu*, more usually known as 'Great Harry'.

This ship was built for war, with over 180 guns

Henry's defences

Henry VIII improved the country's defences and stocked it with up-to-date arms. His own spectacular coats of armour were made by the most skilful armourers. He brought many of these workers from Europe to make suits of armour at his royal workshops in Greenwich. Henry also built the royal naval dockyards at Deptford and Woolwich and expanded the English fleet from a few ships to a sizeable fleet, equipped with heavy cannon. Along the south coast of England, Henry built a series of defensive castles. Many of these castles, including Deal and Walmer in Kent, and St Mawes near Falmouth, still stand today.

▶ Deal Castle in Kent was one of the forts built by Henry VIII to protect the English south coast against invasion.

The fort is surrounded by a curtain wall

There was a moat between the curtain wall and the fort

The low-rise style was a typical design for Henry's forts

*The central **keep** is circular*

The fort has six lobes (semicircles), enclosing the central keep

The Spanish Armada

The biggest military crisis of Elizabeth's reign was the attack by the Spanish Armada (fleet). At that time, Spain controlled the Netherlands, where one of Philip II's generals, the Duke of Parma, had recently crushed a rebellion against Spanish rule. Philip's plan was for Parma's Spanish troops to cross the Channel and attack England. The Armada was to provide cover by distracting attention from the movement of the troops.

The Spanish Armada left Spain on 12 July 1588. On 19 July, the Armada was spotted off the Scilly Islands and the English fleet set out to meet it. Although the English ships were faster than the stately Spanish vessels, they inflicted little damage and the Armada continued up the Channel to Calais. The English took desperate measures.

On the night of 27 July, eight old ships were towed towards the anchored Spanish fleet, then set on fire and cast loose. The Spanish Armada scattered in confusion, the survivors making their escape northwards. Out of 130 ships, only about 67 returned to Spain.

The 'Armada portrait'

The story of the Armada is told in numerous paintings and maps. England's triumph was also captured in a painting of Elizabeth known as the 'Armada portrait'. The painting shows the Queen resplendent in pearls and sumptuous dress. It may have been commissioned by Sir Francis Drake to celebrate England's famous victory. Elizabeth's hand overshadows North America on the globe, indicating England's ambitions in this part of the world.

▶ The splendid 'Armada portrait' of Elizabeth I. In fact, there are three versions of this portrait by various unknown British artists.

This scene shows the English fleet and the fireships

Elizabeth's magnificent pearls display her great wealth

Elizabeth's right hand rests on a globe to show that she is the 'great Empress of the world'

This scene shows the Spanish fleet being tossed by the waves

The arm of the chair is carved in the form of a mermaid. Mermaids were thought to lure sailors to their deaths – just like the Spanish sailors above

Seafaring and exploration

A great age of discovery started in the late 15th century, with the voyage of an Italian sailor who was working for Spain – Christopher Columbus. For centuries, traders had brought silks, spices and other precious goods overland to Europe from the East. By sailing west across the Atlantic Ocean, Columbus believed he could find a sea route to the East. In 1492, he landed in the Caribbean. Although he believed that he had reached the shores of some eastern land, he had discovered a continent unknown to Europeans. Five years later, the English king, Henry VII, gave permission for another Italian sailor, John Cabot, to sail west. Cabot set out from Bristol in 1497 and reached the coast of North America. Like Columbus, he was convinced that he had reached the East, although he found no spices or precious stones. He did, however, report on the vast numbers of cod, and soon English boats were sailing to North America to catch these valuable fish.

As exploration of the **New World** continued, Spain and Portugal laid claim to much of it in a treaty drawn up in 1494. Then, in 1519, Ferdinand Magellan, a Portuguese sailor who was working for the Spanish, set out on what was to be the first expedition to circumnavigate the world. He sailed around the southern tip of South America and into the Pacific Ocean – proving that there was a sea route to the East.

◀ This jewel represents a type of ship used by Portuguese and Spanish sailors in the 15th and 16th centuries – the caravel.

The jewel is made from malachite, a dark green stone, and is decorated with a coloured glassy material called enamel.

The mount is decorated with Tudor designs. It is made from silver covered with a thin layer of gold

▶ The Walsingham bowl. This bowl, seized from a Spanish ship by English sailors, is said to have been a gift from Elizabeth I to Sir Thomas Walsingham, the cousin of her Secretary of State, Sir Francis Walsingham.

The bowl is Chinese Ming Dynasty (1368–1644) porcelain. Luxury goods such as Chinese porcelain were brought from Manila (in the Philippines) to the west coast of the Americas. They were then carried overland to the American east coast and transported by ship to Europe

English expeditions

Throughout the first half of the 16th century, Spain and Portugal led the way in seafaring and exploration. During the reign of Edward VI, an English expedition under Sir Hugh Willoughby and Richard Chancellor tried to find a route to the East (Asia) through a 'northeast passage'. But it was during the reign of Elizabeth I that English sailors really began to make their presence felt on the oceans. There are portraits of the most famous Elizabethan sailors, including Sir Francis Drake, Sir Walter Raleigh and Sir John Hawkins. Control of the seas became part of an ongoing battle with Spain, as Elizabeth licensed her sea captains to attack Spanish ships bringing back gold and other treasure from the New World.

Sir Francis Drake

A portrait of Sir Francis Drake, painted in 1591, shows him standing beside a table on which rests a globe. The globe recalls the fact that Drake was the second person (Magellan was the first) to sail around the world. On board his ship, the *Pelican* (later renamed the *Golden Hind*), he set off from Plymouth in November 1577. He sailed across the Atlantic and through the Strait of Magellan, plundering Spanish settlements and ships as he made his way northwards up the South American coast. His journey across the Pacific took him to the Spice Islands (in present-day Indonesia). He returned to England in 1580, and was knighted by Elizabeth on board the *Golden Hind* in the following year.

This is Drake's coat of arms (family symbol)

The translation of Drake's motto is 'Great things arise from small'

The globe refers to Drake's circumnavigation of the world

◀ This portrait of Sir Francis Drake was painted by Marcus Gheeraerts the Younger.

The jewel hanging from Drake's belt is a locket containing a miniature portrait of Queen Elizabeth, painted by Nicholas Hilliard. It is said to have been presented to Drake in 1581 on board his ship, the Golden Hind, when he was knighted by Elizabeth

New trade

Sir Hugh Willoughby and Richard Chancellor did not find a sea route to the East on their expedition of 1553. In fact, Willoughby and his crew died during the voyage, but Chancellor returned with news that he had opened up trade with a new country – Muscovy (Russia). Soon English cloth was being exported to Muscovy, while Russian furs, animal hides and tallow (used to make candles) were brought back to England. Attempts to open up trade with the East continued in the 1570s and 1580s. Martin Frobisher led the search for the route through the north of America known as the 'northwest passage'. But, despite several voyages by Frobisher and by John Davis, nothing of any commercial value was found.

Elizabethan sailors were keen to find a trade route to the East because spices from the East were much sought-after in Elizabethan times. They were used to flavour food and drink, as well as in medicines. In the 1580s, an overland trade route to the East was opened up by Ralph Fitch, who travelled to India.

▼ This nutmeg grater dates from the middle of the 17th century. Nutmeg from the Spice Islands was used in Tudor times for the warmed spiced wine that was served at court celebrations.

The case is decorated with Tudor roses

The nutmeg grater and case are made from silver

▶ This woodcut shows the preparation and cooking of meat. Spices were often used to disguise the flavour of meat that was less than fresh.

Fitch's journey led to the founding of a trading company called the English East India Company in 1600.

New colonies

The new Spanish colonies in Central and South America brought huge wealth to Philip II of Spain. In the 1570s and 1580s, Humphrey Gilbert and Sir Walter Raleigh drew up plans to establish English colonies in parts of North America unclaimed by the Spanish. Several attempts by Gilbert to establish a colony failed, and Gilbert himself was drowned in 1583. Two years later, Raleigh sent out the first group of English settlers, including the artist John White, to Roanoke Island, off the coast of Virginia. White drew detailed pictures of the local people, their settlements, and the wildlife. The settlers abandoned Roanoke in 1586, but a year later a second group of settlers was led by John White himself. This expedition also failed.

▶ *The Village of Secoton, West Virginia.* This engraving by Theodore de Bry was made from an original drawing by John White. It was included in de Bry's *America*, which was published in 1590, with text by John Harriot, the scientific adviser for the 1585 colony.

Trade and piracy

In 1562, John Hawkins sailed to West Africa and bought slaves. He took these black slaves to the new Spanish colonies in the Caribbean and sold them. The voyage made a profit, and he repeated it two years later. However, Philip II of Spain complained that Hawkins was breaking the strict laws which prevented Spanish colonists from trading with English merchants. On his third voyage, Hawkins was accompanied by Sir Francis Drake. This time, their ships were attacked by the Spanish. Both Hawkins and Drake limped home. Hawkins never sailed to the Caribbean again, while Drake spent the next 20 years attacking Spanish colonies and ships, bringing back Spanish treasure to England. His actions were those of a pirate, but he soon became a hero in his home country.

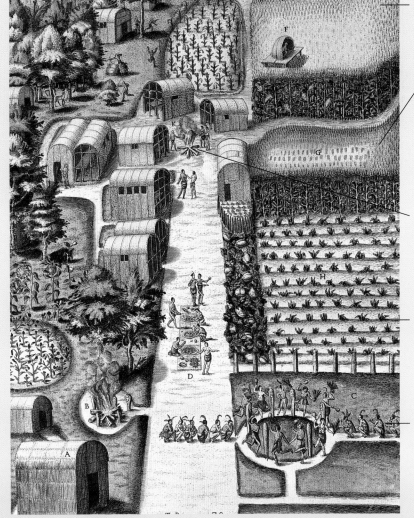

A field of ripe corn

A field of green corn

The engraving shows the different activities going on in the native American village

A field of newly planted corn

A ceremonial dance

Portrait painting

Portrait painting was a feature of the Tudor period. Many painters came from abroad to work at the courts of the Tudor monarchs. The most famous was Hans Holbein the Younger, who was court painter for Henry VIII. Others included Levina Teerlinc, Hans Eworth, William Scrots and Antonio Moro, all from the Netherlands. Levina Teerlinc came to England in 1546. She was a court painter for Mary I and also made several miniature and full-size portraits of Elizabeth I (see the Maundy Service picture on page 18). William Scrots was court painter to Edward VI, while Hans Eworth worked for Mary I. Antonio Moro was sent to England by Philip II in 1554 to paint his new wife, Mary I (see portrait on page 14), although he did not stay in England.

Hans Holbein the Younger

The German painter Hans Holbein came to England in 1526 as a guest of the statesman and humanist scholar Sir Thomas More. Holbein settled in England in 1532 and became court painter to Henry VIII. He painted many portraits of the leading members of Henry's court, as well as of the King and his family. He was also sent abroad by Henry to paint portraits of possible wives for the King. Holbein's picture of Anne of Cleves persuaded Henry to send for her to be his fourth wife. They married in 1540 but Henry was so disappointed with the real Anne that the marriage lasted only six months before Henry divorced her. Holbein continued to paint for the King, dying of the plague in 1543.

▼ Anne of Cleves by Hans Holbein. This was the portrait that persuaded Henry VIII to send for her to be his wife. A contemporary description of Anne of Cleves described her as 'of middling beauty, with a determined and resolute countenance…'

Nicholas Hilliard

Unlike Henry VIII, Edward VI and Mary I, Elizabeth did not employ a court painter. The most talented artist to paint the Queen was probably Nicholas Hilliard. Hilliard specialized in miniature paintings with exquisitely fine details. These small paintings were mounted in beautiful cases and frames, and were often worn like jewels. Hilliard painted many miniatures of the Queen. He is also the probable artist of two large-scale pictures of Elizabeth, the 'Pelican portrait' (see page 16) and the 'Phoenix portrait', both named after jewels that Elizabeth wears in the pictures.

Christina of Denmark

In 1538, Holbein travelled to Brussels. His job was to paint a 16-year-old widow, Christina of Denmark. He had been sent by Henry VIII, who was interested in marrying Christina. Holbein had only three hours with his subject. He could not complete a full-length portrait in this short time, so instead he made a sketch of Christina and probably took notes about the colour of her skin, her hair and her clothes. He then painted the portrait in his London workshop. Although Henry liked what he saw, the match between him and Christina did not go any further.

▶ This miniature of Elizabeth I playing the lute is by Nicholas Hilliard.

When it was first painted, this miniature would have sparkled because Hilliard used a silver pigment (which has turned black over the course of time) on Elizabeth's dress

She plucks the strings of the lute with her right hand

Elizabeth is seated on a throne

Elizabeth was an accomplished musician, and she played the lute throughout her life, both for private pleasure and in front of an admiring audience

The original oval picture measures 4.8 by 3.9 centimetres

Everyday life

Paintings give us a huge amount of information about life in Tudor England. However, only wealthy families could afford to have portraits painted so we have to look elsewhere to learn about the lives of ordinary people. Manuals on subjects such as household management, education or gardening were often illustrated with black-and-white **woodcuts**. Furniture and other household items have also survived to give us a picture of how people lived.

New foods

Voyagers to the **New World** brought back gold, silver and other treasure. They also brought new foods never before seen in Europe. For example, turkeys were first brought to England in the 1520s. Sweetcorn, potatoes, tomatoes, peanuts, pineapples, vanilla, chocolate and peppers were other introductions. It is said that it was Sir Francis Drake who brought the potato to England, in the late 16th century.

Family life

Wealthy, upper-class families tended to have more children than ordinary families. This was because they usually married at a younger age, and were probably better fed. However, in all families the death rate for children was high. Babies were swaddled – wrapped tightly with strips of woollen material, and sometimes even bound to boards. Swaddling for the first few months of life was meant to encourage the arms and legs to grow straight. Babies were breastfed until the age of three or four, when they began to eat solid food. Boys and girls were dressed identically until boys were 'breeched' – put into 'breeches' or trousers – at the age of five or six.

This woman is thought to be Lord Cobham's sister — *Lord Cobham* — *The eldest boy has been 'breeched'* — *Lady Cobham*

▲ This painting shows William Brooke, 10th Lord Cobham, and his family in 1567. Lord and Lady Cobham's six children were born within the first seven years of their marriage.

Children learned to stand and walk with the help of wooden walking frames and leather leading strings which seem to have been very similar to the equipment used for babies today. Children's toys included hobby-horses, drums, kites, popguns and rattles. Many families also possessed a **hornbook** to help children learn their alphabet.

◄ Children playing games in the Long Gallery at Knole, Kent.

Work

The vast majority of ordinary people worked either as farm labourers, in trades such as building or weaving, or as domestic servants. Wages were paid and rents were due four times a year on the 'quarter-days' – Lady Day (25 March), Midsummer Day (24 June), Michaelmas (29 September) and Christmas. Woodcuts from manuals give us information about the types of tools used for farming, and for other trades.

Furniture

Much furniture survives from the Tudor period. Clothes were kept in 'presses' or wardrobes, while chests were used to store linen. In wealthier houses, four-poster beds were hung with curtains that could be drawn at night to keep draughts out. Chairs were quite unusual items – people mostly sat on long benches, chests or stools. Large wooden chairs with arms were reserved for important people, and a very few of these were upholstered to make them more comfortable.

▶ Known as the Great Bed of Ware, because it was originally at the White Hart Inn in Ware, this bed dates from the reign of Elizabeth I. It was famous in its own day because of its size.

Originally, the woodwork on the bed would have been brightly painted

The bed measures 3.4 metres by 3.0 metres. It was built by a Hertfordshire carpenter, Jonas Fosbrooke

Costume and fashion

Portraits of Tudor nobles show us how fashions changed throughout the period. We know about the less sumptuous clothes worn by ordinary people from images in manuals and from finds such as the clothing preserved on the sunken Tudor battleship, the *Mary Rose*.

Court fashions

The elaborate costume worn by court ladies during the Tudor period required a great deal of time, and some help, to put on. Typically, a noblewoman wore a simple smock or shift as an undergarment, with stockings that came to the knee and were held up with ribbon. On top of this was a corset stiffened with reed or whalebone and a stiffened underskirt called a farthingale. Later in the Tudor period, court dress changed to include new fashions such as the wheel farthingale. This type of skirt, with a large wheel-shaped frame beneath, can be clearly seen in the painting of Elizabeth I in procession (see page 16).

Her headdress is the gable or kennel type

The large cuffs of the gown are pinned back to show false sleeves

Her dress has a low-cut, square neckline

▶ This portrait of Jane Seymour was painted by Hans Holbein around the time of her wedding to Henry VIII.

The V-shaped opening of her red velvet gown reveals an embroidered underskirt or kirtle

The sleeves are slashed and the lining is pulled through

Slashing involved cutting slits in the outer material and pulling the lining through. It was even more popular in men's clothing than in women's. A painting of Henry VIII by Holbein (see page 10) shows just how elaborate a powerful man's dress could be. Henry's red velvet gown was embroidered with gold cord and lined with fur. Beneath his gown he wore a doublet, or close-fitting jacket, which fell to just above the knee and opened at the front. It was encrusted with jewels and embroidery. Henry also wore stockings, and shoes with leather or cork soles.

Everyday clothes

Clothes worn by ordinary people were, of course, far less extravagant. An illustration showing middle-class women with their servant from a *Description of England* gives us information about the type of clothes worn in the late 16th century. All the women wear simple ruffs – starched lace collars which stood high around the neck. Extremely elaborate ruffs were worn by noblewomen during the reign of Elizabeth I (see portrait of Elizabeth on page 21). Meanwhile, a servant wears a simple gown with an apron, and a type of hat called a *copotain*.

▶ This brown leather jerkin dates from the middle of the 16th century.

The *Mary Rose*

The *Mary Rose* was one of Henry VIII's favourite warships and was named after his sister Mary. It was built in 1509–11 and had a distinguished record when it accidentally sank in the Solent, off the Isle of Wight, during a skirmish with the French fleet. The wreck of the *Mary Rose* was raised in 1982. Remains of clothes preserved in the mud of the sea-bed give us some insight into what was worn by the sailors. There are leather jerkins (sleeveless tops), some of which were slashed like the clothes worn by Henry VIII. There are also some shoes, two leather mittens and a velvet hat.

The buttons are made from pewter (a type of metal)

The jerkin is decorated with heart and star motifs which have been punched into the leather

31

Education

In Tudor times, most children were educated by their parents. Boys were taught what they needed to know to be a farmer, or to work in a trade, while girls learned how to run a house. Sometimes parents also taught their children the basics of reading and writing. Some children, mostly boys, did go to school. Such boys were destined for a career in the Church, or as teachers, lawyers or book-keepers, and for these jobs they needed to be able to read, write and count.

▼ This woodcut shows a schoolmaster and his pupils. It is dated around 1560.

Grammar schools

Before the Tudor period, most schools were run by the Catholic Church. Their main purpose was to train their pupils for a life in the Church. During the Tudor period, many grammar schools were established in towns across the country. These were secular schools (not run by the Church), and many were founded by wealthy noblemen or merchants. Many of these schools are still in existence today, and some continue to make use of their original Tudor buildings.

The birch was used for beatings for misbehaviour

The pupils are divided into two groups, perhaps to do different activities

The pupils sit on long benches, or 'forms'

In London, St Paul's School was founded in 1509 by the humanist scholar John Colet. Colet was a friend of Erasmus, and he was convinced that education was an important way to improve society. He wrote: 'my intent is by this school specially to increase knowledge and worshipping of God and Our Lord Christ Jesu and good Christian life and manners in the children'. St Paul's became a model for other grammar schools of the period, which included Shrewsbury School (founded 1551), Repton School (founded 1557) and Rugby School (founded 1567).

▼ This school in Steyning, West Sussex, dates from Tudor times, although it did not become a grammar school until 1614. Like many Tudor schools it was a 'school for little boys'.

Girls' education

The role of women in Tudor society was to run a household and bring up children. Mothers educated their daughters to take on this role from an early age. Many girls were taught to read, either at small local schools or at home. They also learned to sew, practising the various different stitches on small pieces of cloth called samplers.

In the grammar schools, boys usually received a **Classical** education, learning how to read, write and speak in Latin and sometimes Greek. Often several classes were taught in one large room, making these crowded and noisy places. Some of these pupils went on to university at Oxford or Cambridge, where they studied subjects such as grammar, logic, **rhetoric** and philosophy.

Hornbooks

Many educational manuals were published during the Tudor period, giving us information about what children were taught and how they were taught. Hornbooks were used to teach children how to read. A hornbook was a piece of wood in the shape of a small bat. A piece of paper with the alphabet and other reading exercises was pasted on one side. The paper was covered with a thin layer of horn for protection. These books were often used by many generations.

▼ Hornbooks contained the basics for learning to read.

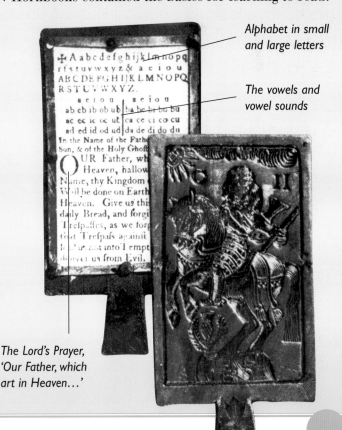

Alphabet in small and large letters

The vowels and vowel sounds

The Lord's Prayer, 'Our Father, which art in Heaven...'

Popular entertainments

Favourite pastimes during the Tudor period included bear- and bull-baiting and cockfights, as well as bowls, card games, wrestling and football. Bear- and bull-baiting were cruel sports in which the tethered animal was attacked by a fierce dog. Only nobles were allowed to take part in some forms of entertainment, including hunting on horseback, real tennis and **jousting**. Real tennis was played in a special indoor court and was a particular favourite of Henry VII. His son, Henry VIII, also loved real tennis as well as hunting and jousting, while Elizabeth I liked to watch bear-baiting.

We know about ordinary people's pastimes from illustrations of everyday life in manuals and other books – usually **woodcuts**. However, most people had limited opportunities to play sport or watch entertainment. A law of 1512 banned playing cards, skittles, bowls or dice for most of the year – it was feared these games would encourage gambling. In 1585, Parliament tried to stop the cruel sport of bear-baiting, but was over-ruled by Elizabeth I.

▼ The cruel sports of bull- and bear-baiting were popular in Tudor times.

The spectators watch the events in the courtyard below

The bull is taunted by dogs

The bear is chained to a post

Players and plays

From medieval times, travelling players had performed plays in inn-yards, town squares and private houses. The plays were usually performed to celebrate Christian festivals. The first permanent stage was established at the Red Lion in Whitechapel in 1567, and nine years later the first theatre was built in Shoreditch, beginning a golden age of Elizabethan theatre. Many new theatres were built, mostly outside the City of London because of the disapproval of the Mayor and Corporation. The travelling players' companies were also very popular at court. Some of the companies' names – such as the Lord Chamberlain's Men, the Earl of Leicester's Men and the Queen's Men – show that they had the support of powerful members of the nobility.

▼A scene from William Shakespeare's play *Titus Andronicus*. This sketch was probably made in 1594 by the actor Henry Peacham.

There is only one contemporary image of the interior of an Elizabethan theatre. This picture, of the Swan, was copied from a sketch made in 1596 by Johannes de Witt. The accuracy of the sketch has been questioned when compared to descriptions of theatres of the time, and to evidence collected from excavations at the sites of the Rose and Globe theatres in London. William Shakespeare, the leading playwright of the period, wrote many of his plays for performance at the Globe theatre by the Lord Chamberlain's Men. A contemporary sketch of one of his plays shows a mixture of costume, suggesting that historical accuracy was not a high priority for the actors.

Football

Football was popular during Tudor times – but not as we know it today. There was no limit to the number of players that could take part, and the goalposts were set about a mile (1.6 kilometres) apart. According to one contemporary description it was 'more a fight than a game' and many people were injured as a result of playing it. The game was officially banned in 1540.

The other characters are in Elizabethan dress

This character wears a Roman toga

Gardens

Before the Tudor period, many large gardens were attached to monasteries or nunneries, where monks or nuns grew a wide variety of fruit, vegetables, herbs and flowers. A typical medieval garden was a square or rectangular shape, enclosed on all four sides by walls.

The practice of enclosing gardens continued into the Tudor period. But during the 16th century, people in France and then England began to copy the gardens of **Renaissance** Italy, and garden design became much grander. Henry VII laid out large gardens at his palace in Richmond, but it was under Henry VIII that gardens became important symbols of the wealth and power of the monarchy.

Heraldic beasts

Important features of the gardens of Henry VIII were **heraldic** beasts such as lions, dragons, greyhounds, antelopes and horses. The beasts were carved from wood, painted and mounted on wooden poles. They lined the walks of the garden, and at Hampton Court were connected by fences painted in the Tudor colours of white and green.

▼ The Pond Gardens at Hampton Court today. Henry VIII's Renaissance gardens were replaced by later monarchs, notably Charles II and William and Mary, with new designs.

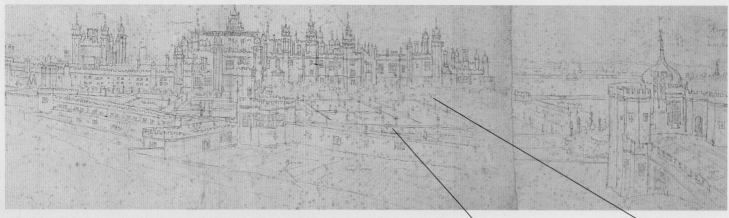

▲ A panorama of Hampton Court and its gardens as seen from the River Thames in 1555. The drawing is by Anthonis van den Wyngaerde.

The Privy Garden was decorated with heraldic beasts mounted on poles

The Tudor part of Hampton Court Palace was built from 1514 onwards

Elizabethan gardens

Elizabeth did not build royal palaces as her father had done. Instead, she relied on her courtiers to build grand houses and design lavish gardens to reflect her glory as queen. When Elizabeth was on a royal progress, the houses in which she stayed had to meet her requirements. Similarly, the gardens attached to these great houses were designed as tributes to the Queen. The Great Gardens of Theobalds, built by Elizabeth's minister William Cecil, were enormous and surrounded by decorative canals. The gardens at Nonsuch Palace, which had been sold during the reign of Mary I, were altered during Elizabeth's reign. Lord Lumley, the new owner, erected a fountain with a statue of the Roman goddess Diana at its centre. People of the time understood this as a tribute to their queen. Diana was the Roman goddess of the moon and of hunting. She also symbolized chastity and modesty, and was often used by painters and poets to describe and praise Queen Elizabeth.

Knots and mazes

Another important feature of Henry's royal gardens was pattern. When Henry stood at an upper window in Hampton Court or Nonsuch Palace, he looked down on a chess-board effect of squares, each square divided into elaborate patterns. These squares were called knots. The pattern of the knot was laid out in plants such as rosemary, thyme or lavender. The spaces between the plants were sometimes filled with different-coloured earths and sands, sometimes with flowers in blocks of contrasting colours. The maze was a development of the knot. A maze was big enough for people to walk along its paths, divided by hedges, in search of the route that led to the centre of the maze.

▼ A bird's-eye view of an Elizabethan garden from *The Gardener's Labyrinth* of 1571.

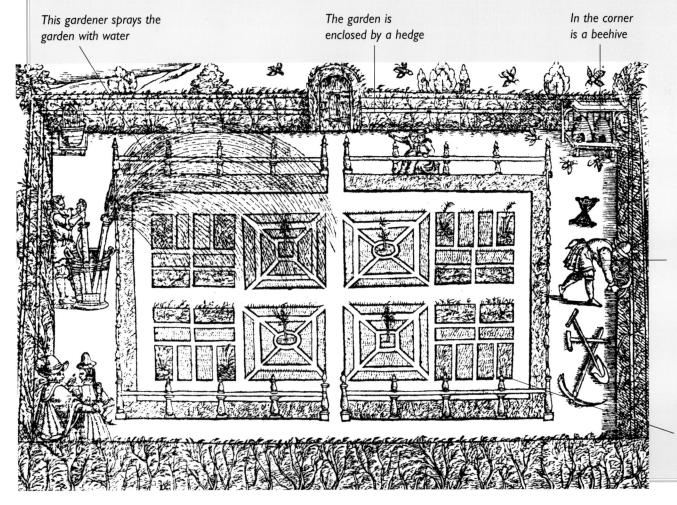

This gardener sprays the garden with water

The garden is enclosed by a hedge

In the corner is a beehive

This gardener is hard at work with a small scythe, trimming the hedge. His other tools lie on the path next to him

The garden is divided into patterned sections, called knots

Literature and music

During the reign of Elizabeth I, there was a remarkable flowering of literature and music in England. This period saw the work of poets such as Sir Philip Sidney and Edmund Spenser, and musicians such as William Byrd and Thomas Tallis.

Poetry

The Queen was the central focus of much Elizabethan poetry. Elizabeth encouraged poets to celebrate her reign and the poet Edmund Spenser wrote a long poem (uncompleted at his death in 1599) called *The Faerie Queene*. In it Spenser linked the fairy world in his poem to the real-life world of Elizabeth's court, celebrating Elizabeth as Gloriana.

Spenser received fifty pounds from the Queen on the publication of *The Faerie Queene* but died in poverty.

Another major literary figure in Elizabeth's court was Sir Philip Sidney. As well as a poet, he was a soldier and a statesman, and this is reflected in his portrait. To the Elizabethan public, Sidney was the ideal courtier. He wrote the first sequence of **sonnets** in the English language (*Astrophel and Stella*), as well as a long **prose** work called *Arcadia*.

◄ This portrait of Sir Philip Sidney, dressed in the stiff and formal Spanish style, is by an unknown English artist of the 16th century.

The sleeve is slashed in highly fashionable style

The front is shaped in a 'peascod belly' style

His doublet is stuffed with material called bombast (made from rags, horsehair and cotton) to fill it out and remove any creases

The close-fitting sleeves end in wrist ruffs

He wears highly decorated trunk hose, also stuffed with bombast to give them shape

Music

Music was very important at the Tudor court, and both Henry VIII and Elizabeth I were accomplished musicians. Paintings show Elizabeth playing the **lute**, while Henry wrote several pieces that still survive today. Music was important in church, too. In the religious settlement of 1559 (see page 43), Elizabeth kept the tradition of cathedral choirs and music during church services. Her Masters of Music at the Royal Chapel, Thomas Tallis followed by William Byrd, wrote music for the new **Protestant** services, in English.

Like poets, composers celebrated Elizabeth in their music. A sequence of madrigals (part-songs for three to five voices) called *The Triumphs of Oriana* was edited by the composer Thomas Morley, praising Elizabeth as Oriana. Each of the 29 madrigals was written by a different composer, and each one ended with the words 'Long live fair Oriana'. Unfortunately, although the date on the title page is 1601, the collection was not published until 1603 – by which time the Queen was dead.

Utopia

One of the leading humanists in Tudor England was Sir Thomas More. More was a lawyer who became Lord Chancellor to Henry VIII. He refused to recognize Henry's marriage to Anne Boleyn, and Henry had him executed in 1535. More's best-known work, *Utopia*, describes an imaginary island where there is an ideal society run on humanist lines, featuring free state education and tolerance of all religions. The name came from the Greek words *ou* and *topos*, meaning 'no place'. *Utopia* was first published in Latin, in 1516. It was translated into English in 1551.

▼ This woodcut for Thomas More's *Utopia* is by Ambrosius Holbein, elder brother of Hans Holbein the Younger.

'Fons Anydri' is the source of the River Anydrus (meaning 'Waterless')

The capital Amaurotum (meaning 'Mist-town') lies in the centre of the island

'Ostium Anydri' is the mouth of the River Anydrus

Religion

The **Reformation** started as a protest movement against the Roman Catholic Church – the name '**Protestant**' initially referred to someone who 'protested'. In the late 15th century, some people in Europe began to question the practices of the Catholic Church, its power and its wealth. In 1517, a German monk called Martin Luther attacked the corruption of the Catholic Church and suggested various reforms. He attracted enough followers to set up a separate church, which became known as the Protestant Church.

The break with Rome

In England, people discussed the new religious ideas. Some turned to the Protestant Church, although this was dangerous because if they were found out they could be burned as **heretics**. Henry VIII disapproved of Protestant reforms and even wrote a book against Luther – for which he was honoured by the **Pope**. But the Pope refused to end Henry's marriage to Catherine of Aragon.

▼ The title page to the Great Bible, *The Byble in Englyshe*, first published in 1539.

Henry VIII hands out Verbum Dei ('The Word of God') to Thomas Cranmer, Archbishop of Canterbury, and Thomas Cromwell, Henry's chief minister

God is shown in the clouds above Henry

Cranmer and Cromwell, who supported Protestantism, are shown distributing copies of the English Bible to the bishops and nobility

The Bible is being read to the ordinary people

The people cry, 'Vivat Rex' ('Long live the King')

The King then took matters into his own hands. In 1534, he declared himself Supreme Head of the Church in England, and broke off all relations with the Pope and Rome. Henry's actions did not mean that he became a Protestant. He continued to worship at Catholic services which were said in Latin. But he did allow some reforms to the Anglican (English) Church, including the use of an English Bible.

Closing down the monasteries

In 1536, Henry and his minister Thomas Cromwell turned their attentions to the Catholic monasteries. The royal treasury was empty and Cromwell saw that the great wealth of the monasteries would provide a solution to the need for money. The King, as Head of the Church, ordered that the monasteries be 'dissolved' or closed. This process started in 1536 with the smaller monasteries, and by 1540 all the monasteries in England were shut down. Most of the monks and nuns were given pensions. All the buildings, money and possessions that had belonged

to the monasteries became the property of the King. The ruins of many of the monastery buildings still stand today.

Translations of the Bible

In 1539, Henry authorized the use of the Great Bible. This was the first time that the Bible was read in English in churches. Before this time, most people relied on priests to explain the Bible to them. Only those who understood Latin or Greek were able to read the Bible for themselves. Translations of the Bible into English were banned – although some handwritten versions did exist. Henry's Great Bible was based on two earlier translations into English made by William Tyndale and Miles Coverdale. Tyndale managed to have his English translation of the New Testament published in 1525 in Cologne in Germany. However, he was captured and executed for heresy in 1536. Coverdale published his translation of the complete Bible in Zurich, Switzerland, in 1535.

▼ The ruins of Fountains Abbey, founded in 1132, in Yorkshire. Life in the abbey came to an end in 1539, as a result of Henry VIII's dissolution of the monasteries.

The abbey buildings were left empty and were soon stripped of their valuable window glass and roof lead

The abbey and its land were sold by the King to a merchant called Robert Gresham

Protestant reforms

When Edward VI came to the throne in 1547, he was only nine years old, and the real power fell into the hands of Edward's **Protector**, the Duke of Somerset. Between them, Edward and Somerset began turning England into a Protestant country.

In 1549, Somerset introduced a Book of Common Prayer, written by Thomas Cranmer. It set out church services in English for the first time (Catholic services were in Latin). In the same year, an **Act** of Uniformity was passed which stated that the Book of Common Prayer was to be used in every church in England. As a result, it became illegal to use Catholic forms of worship. The Book of Common Prayer and the Act of Uniformity sparked off riots in Cornwall.

At the same time, the last traces of the Catholic faith were destroyed in churches all over the country. Protestants believed that people should worship God directly, not through prayers to the saints or other figures. They thought that paintings and statues in churches tempted people to worship these images rather than the one God. During Edward's reign, many church paintings were whitewashed and sculptures were smashed.

▼ *Edward VI and the Pope: An Allegory of the Reformation.* This extraordinary picture was painted by an unknown artist around 1570.

Edward VI, the boy-king, sits at the centre of the picture on his throne

Protector Somerset stands to the right of Edward VI

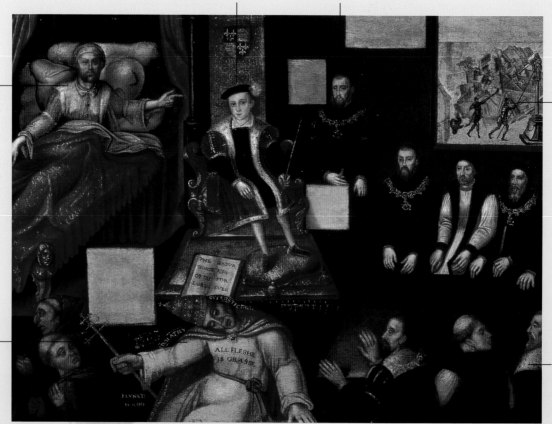

Henry VIII points to his successor from his death-bed

In the background, idols and images are being destroyed

The Pope is shown as a broken man, languishing at Edward's feet. Henry and Edward have overthrown the corruption of the Roman Catholic Church

Members of the Privy Council (advisers appointed by the monarch) sit around the table

Mary and Elizabeth

Mary was a staunch Catholic, and when she became Queen in 1553 she undid the reforms of Edward's reign. Catholic services replaced the Book of Common Prayer, and many Protestants were forced to leave the country. Under Mary's rule, 283 Protestants were burned at the stake for their beliefs – an action which caused widespread anger among Protestants.

When Elizabeth I came to the throne in 1558, people braced themselves for more upheaval. In 1559, a settlement was made which kept some of the ceremony of the Catholic Church while returning to the Protestant services in Cranmer's Book of Common Prayer. England became a Protestant country once more, and Catholics were fined for refusing to attend Protestant services.

Foxe's *Book of Martyrs*

John Foxe was a Protestant priest from Lincolnshire. During the reign of Edward VI, he wrote a book about the Protestants who had died for their faith, linking their fate with the sufferings of the early Christians under the rule of the ancient Romans. When Mary came to the throne, Foxe escaped abroad. He took his book with him and to it he added the people who were burned at the stake by Mary. After Mary's death he returned to England. Foxe's *Book of Martyrs* was first published in English in 1563 (there was a 1559 Latin edition). It was illustrated with vivid pictures of burnings and hangings. Elizabeth ordered that a copy be placed in every cathedral and many churches to remind people of what had happened under a Catholic queen.

▼ This **woodcut** from Foxe's *Book of Martyrs* shows the burning of Thomas Haukes.

The date of Haukes's execution was 10 June 1555. Burning at the stake was a terrible death

O Lord, Receiue my ſpirite.

Images such as this were used to remind people in Elizabethan England of what had happened under a Roman Catholic queen

Timeline

1485
Battle of Bosworth; death of Richard III; Henry VII becomes King

1486
Marriage of Henry VII and Elizabeth of York

1492
Columbus sails to the **New World**

1497
Cabot sails to North America

1509
Death of Henry VII; Henry VIII succeeds to the throne and marries Catherine of Aragon

1517
Luther attacks corruption of **Roman Catholic Church**

1519–22
Magellan's fleet makes first circumnavigation of the world

1520
Meeting at the Field of the Cloth of Gold

1533
Henry VIII marries Anne Boleyn

1534
Henry VIII declares himself Supreme Head of the Church in England and breaks with Rome

1536
Death of Catherine of Aragon; execution of Anne Boleyn; Henry VIII marries Jane Seymour

1536–40
Dissolution of the monasteries

1537
Birth of Edward VI; death of Jane Seymour

1539
Great Bible (in English) authorized for use

1540
Henry VIII marries and divorces Anne of Cleves; marries Catherine Howard

1541
Execution of Catherine Howard

1543
Henry VIII marries Catherine Parr

1547
Death of Henry VIII; Edward VI succeeds to the throne

1549
Introduction of Book of Common Prayer; rebellions in Cornwall and East Anglia

1553
Death of Edward VI; Lady Jane Grey becomes queen for nine days; Mary I succeeds to the throne

1554
Mary I marries King Philip II of Spain

1558
Death of Mary I; Elizabeth I succeeds to the throne

1559
Acts of Supremacy and Allegiance bring religious settlement

1563
Publication of Foxe's *Book of Martyrs*

1568
Mary Queen of Scots flees to England

1569
Catholic uprising in northern England

1577–80
Drake makes second circumnavigation of the world

1587
Execution of Mary Queen of Scots

1588
Defeat of the Spanish Armada

1600
Founding of the English East India Company

1603
Death of Elizabeth I

Glossary

Act law that has been passed by Parliament

Celtic describes the Celts, different groups of people who all spoke Celtic languages and lived throughout Europe. In Tudor Britain the Celts lived mainly in Cornwall and Wales, as well as in Scotland and Ireland

Classical based on the ancient Greek and Roman civilizations

dynasty succession of rulers from the same family, in which power is passed down from one generation to the next

emblem image with a symbolic meaning

heraldic describes images from heraldry, the pictures originally found on the shields of knights to identify them in battle. From the early 12th century, these pictures became badges of honour and were passed down through generations of the same family

heretic someone who has been found guilty of having beliefs contrary to the established (usually Roman Catholic) Church

hornbook piece of wood in the shape of a small bat with a piece of paper pasted on one side showing the alphabet and other reading exercises. The paper was covered with a thin layer of horn for protection

humanism Renaissance movement which celebrated human achievement, and influenced artists and scholars

jousting competition between two mounted riders who galloped towards each other down long lanes, called lists. The riders held long blunt poles, called lances, and the aim was to unseat the opponent

keep large, strong tower in a castle or fort

lute a stringed instrument, with a pear-shaped back, which is held on the lap and plucked

New World name given to the Americas by Europeans after Columbus's voyage of 1492

patron someone who helps an artist, for example by paying them for specific pieces of work

pope head of the Roman Catholic Church

progress stately royal journey from one place to another

prose non-metrical writing – the opposite of poetry

Protector someone who exercises royal authority on behalf of an under-age monarch

Protestant name given to the followers of Martin Luther who 'protested' against what they saw as the corruption of the Roman Catholic Church

Puritan member of a branch of the Protestant Church that started in England during the 1560s. Puritans believed that more reform was needed to move the Anglican Church further from the Roman Catholic Church

Reformation Protestant movement for reform in the Christian Church, which started in Europe in the early 16th century

Renaissance revival in learning and culture that started in Italy in the 14th century and spread northwards across Europe during the 15th and 16th centuries, based on the study of the art and writing of ancient Greece and Rome

rhetoric language of argument and persuasion

Roman Catholic Church Christian Church, led by the pope, that has its headquarters in the Vatican City in Rome

sonnet poem with fourteen lines divided into two sections of eight and six lines, and with a set rhyme scheme

standard flag carried in battle, often bearing the coat of arms of the monarch or a high-ranking noble

tuberculosis disease that often affects the lungs, causing the sufferer to have a high fever and to cough up blood

woodcut image made by cutting away areas of a block of wood to leave a raised design. The design is then inked and pressed on to a sheet of paper

Further resources

Books

Childs, Alan, *The History Detective Investigates: Tudor Theatre* (Hodder Wayland, 2002)

Chrisp, Peter, *The Illustrated World of the Tudors* (Hodder Wayland, 2001)

Clements, Gillian, *Great Events: Spanish Armada* (Watts, 2003)

Cooper, Alison, *The Tudors and Stuarts* (Hodder Wayland, 2001)

Hebditch, Felicity, *Britain through the Ages: Tudors* (Evans, 2003)

Macdonald, Fiona, *Life in Britain: Britain in Tudor Times* (Watts, 2003)

Middleton, Haydn, *People in the Past: Tudor Children* (Heinemann Library, 2003)

Middleton, Haydn, *People in the Past: Tudor Exploration* (Heinemann Library, 2003)

Middleton, Haydn, *People in the Past: Tudor Jobs* (Heinemann Library, 2003)

Middleton, Haydn, *People in the Past: Tudor Rich and Poor* (Heinemann Library, 2003)

Nash, Margaret, *Into the Unknown: The Tudor Explorers John and Sebastian Cabot* (Hodder Wayland, 2001)

Patchett, Fiona, *Usborne History of Britain: Tudors and Stuarts* (Usborne, 2003)

Wood, Richard, *On the Trail of the Tudors in Britain* (Watts, 2000)

Wright, Rachel, *Tudors* (Watts, 2001)

Websites

http://www.tudorlinks.com/index2.html
Useful site for links to all things Tudor on the web
http://www.channel4.com/history/microsites/H/history/guide16/part08.html
Channel 4 'time-traveller's guide' to Tudor life and times
http://www.englishhistory.net/tudor.html
http://www.tudorhistory.org/

Places to visit

Hampton Court Palace, London

Hardwick Hall, Derbyshire

Montacute House, Somerset

Longleat House, Wiltshire

Burghley House, Lincolnshire

Little Moreton Hall, Cheshire

Henry VII's Chapel, Westminster Abbey, London

National Portrait Gallery, London

King's College Chapel, Cambridge

St George's Chapel, Windsor Castle

The *Mary Rose*, Portsmouth

Deal Castle, Kent

Index

Anne of Cleves 26, 44
architecture 12–13
Armada 17, 21, 45

Bible, translations 40, 41, 44
Boleyn, Anne 10, 11, 18, 39, 44
Book of Common Prayer 42, 43, 45

Catherine of Aragon 10–12, 14, 19, 40, 44
Caxton, William 5
Chancellor, Richard 23, 24
Columbus, Christopher 22, 44
court 18–19
Cranmer, Thomas, Archbishop of Canterbury 15, 40, 43
Cromwell, Thomas 18, 40

Deal Castle 20
Drake, Sir Francis 21, 23, 25, 28, 45

East India Company 25, 45
education 32–3
Edward IV, King 8, 9
Elizabeth of York 4, 9, 44
entertainment 34–5
Erasmus, Desiderius 5
exploration 22–5, 28

family life 28–9
fashion 30–1, 38
Field of the Cloth of Gold 11, 20, 44
Fountains Abbey, Yorkshire 41
Foxe, John, 43, 45

games 34, 35
gardens 36–7
Gheeraerts, Marcus, the Younger 7, 23
Great Bed of Ware 29
Grey, Lady Jane 14, 45

Hampton Court Palace 12, 36, 37
Hawkins, Sir John 23, 25
Henry VI, King 12
Hilliard, Nicholas 19, 23, 27
Holbein, Hans, the Younger 6, 10, 18, 26, 27, 30, 31
houses, Elizabethan 12, 13, 29
Howard, Catherine 44
humanism 4–5

King's College, Cambridge 9, 11, 12

literature 38–9
Luther, Martin 40, 44

Magellan, Ferdinand 22, 44
Mary Queen of Scots 17, 45
monasteries 41, 44
More, Sir Thomas 18, 26, 39
music 38–9

Nonsuch Palace 5, 13, 37
Northumberland, Duke of 14, 15

Parr, Catherine 44
Philip II, King of Spain 14, 15, 17, 21, 25, 26
poetry 38

Protestants 40, 42–3

Raleigh, Sir Walter 23, 25
religion 40–3
Renaissance 4–5
Richard III, King 4, 8, 9, 12, 32, 44

schools 32–3
seafaring 22–3
Seymour, Jane 10, 11, 30, 44, 45
Shakespeare, William 35
ships 17, 20, 23, 30, 31
Sidney, Sir Philip 38
Somerset House 15
Somerset, Duke of 14, 15, 42
Spenser, Edmund 38

Teerlinc, Levina 18, 26
theatres 35
Theobalds, Great Gardens 37
toys 29

Walsingham bowl 22
warfare 20–1
Wars of the Roses 9
Westminster Abbey (Henry VII Chapel) 8, 12
White, John 25
Whitehall Palace 10
Willoughby, Sir Hugh 23, 24
Windsor Castle, St George's Chapel 12
Wolsey, Cardinal 6, 11, 12, 19
work 29

Titles in the *History in Art* series include:

Hardback   1 844 43369 2

Hardback   1 844 43361 7

Hardback   1 844 43359 5

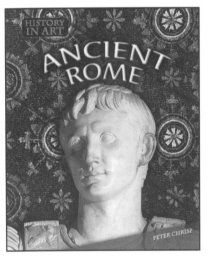

Hardback   1 844 43360 9

Hardback   1 844 43362 5

Hardback   1 844 43370 6

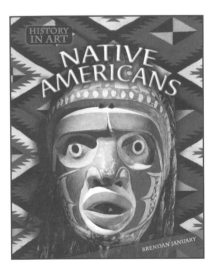

Hardback   1 844 43371 4

Hardback   1 844 43372 2

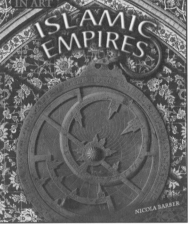

Hardback   1 844 43373 0

Find out about the other titles in this series on our website www.raintreepublishers.co.uk